SOMETIMES I DREAM THAT

I AM NOT

WALT WHITMAN

PREVIOUS BOOKS OF POETRY BY JOSEPH HARRISON

Shakespeare's Horse (2015)
Identity Theft (2008)
Someone Else's Name (2003)
The Fly in the Ointment (1994; published 2014)
The Imposition of Ashes (1987; published 2016)

MORE PRAISE FOR

SOMETIMES I DREAM THAT I AM NOT WALT WHITMAN

"In his brilliant, entertaining, dark, and companionable new book, Joseph Harrison, one of American poetry's best kept secrets, channels the voices and spirits of dead poets as wide ranging and diverse as Mark Strand, Emily Dickinson, Robert Frost, Wallace Stevens and Walt Whitman himself. But Harrison never merely ventriloquizes these and other voices; or if he does the ventriloquism, as he implies in his amazing sequence, 'The Compromised Ventriloquist', is reciprocal—such that, as he says elsewhere in the book, 'every transformation/ becomes another act of self-creation.' This book obliterates the dichotomies of self-expression and impersonality, personal disclosure and self-effacement, tradition and innovation. In the place of such facile and misleading oppositions Harrison has written a book that engages the particularities of our moment with a hawk's eye view of linguistic, metrical and cultural history. The imagination that animates these poems is intimate and vatic, prophetic and mundane, scientific and fantastic; the music is all his own yet everyone's, 'dark and deep / And cold as interstellar night' while unforgettably humane. I love this book."

– Alan Shapiro

MORE PRAISE FOR

SOMETIMES I DREAM THAT I AM NOT WALT WHITMAN

"His suite of cannily resonant imitations of the good gray poet notwithstanding, Joseph Harrison is indeed not Walt Whitman, nor does he seek to be, but his verse responds eloquently to the ardent prediction in *Democratic Vistas* that the 'highest poems' to come would spring from 'the assumption that the process of reading is … in the highest sense, an exercise, a gymnast's struggle.' Harrison's intensely wrought poems reward the reader well beyond the demands they make. Ebullient yet concentrated products of an audacious prosodist and syntactician, an exhilarating logophile and a master of tone, they evince a maker's maker. A set of poems in Emily Dickinson's mode balances the Whitman suite, and Frost and Stevens, Yeats and Auden and Merrill ghost happily through this volume, itself a 'unity of network.' It compasses 'structures of posed placidity'—structures that arise, we come to know, from an 'intemperate liquidity / Whose outbursts, unpredictable, reveal / A flare for the dramatic.'"

– Stephen Yenser

SOMETIMES I DREAM THAT I AM NOT WALT WHITMAN

JOSEPH HARRISON

WAYWISER

First published in 2020 by

THE WAYWISER PRESS

Christmas Cottage, Church Enstone, Chipping Norton, Oxfordshire, OX7 4NN, UK
P.O. Box 6205, Baltimore, MD 21206, USA
https://waywiser-press.com

Editor-in-Chief
Philip Hoy

Senior American Editor
Joseph Harrison

Associate Editors
Eric McHenry | Dora Malech | V. Penelope Pelizzon | Clive Watkins
Greg Williamson | Matthew Yorke

Copyright © Joseph Harrison, 2020

The right of Joseph Harrison to be identified as the author of this work
has been asserted by him in accordance with the
Copyright, Designs and Patents Act of 1988.

All rights reserved. No part of this publication may be reproduced, stored in
a retrieval system, or transmitted in any form or by any means, electronic,
mechanical, photocopying, recording, or otherwise, without the prior permission
of both the copyright owner and the above publisher of this book.

9 7 5 3 1 2 4 6 8

A CIP catalogue record for this book is available from the British Library.

PB ISBN 978-1-904130-98-7
HB ISBN 978-1-911379-00-3

Printed and bound by
T. J. International Ltd., Padstow, Cornwall, PL28 8RW

Acknowledgments

Alabama Literary Review: "Stopping," "Hardy's Writing Trousers," "The Forsaken Singer," "Late Autumnal"

The American Scholar: "Sometimes I Dream that I Am Not Walt Whitman," "Let Them Say Whatever They Want," "Returning to the Sea-shore," "I Hear It Is Charged against Me," "Like a Ghost I Returned," "Some Tuesdays I Go to Lisbon," "My Old Camerado, My Body"

The Antioch Review: "Giotto in Padua"

Birmingham Poetry Review: "Runaway Blimp," "The Retreat"

The Hopkins Review: "The Albatross," "Cézanne in Baltimore"

The Hudson Review: "Song of the NRA," "The Ekphrastic Poet"

Literary Matters: "The Compromised Ventriloquist"

The New Criterion: "Dickens on Fire"

The New York Review of Books: "Mark Strand"

Parnassus: "Derecho," "Echolocation"

Le Parole e le Cose (online): "Velázquez in Rome"

Passager: "My Sister Cut Me into Pieces"

Raritan: "Orogenesis," "Autopoiesis," "The Demon Dinanukht"

Smartish Pace: "The End Was Over," "Coulrophobia with Line from Auden"

The Yale Review: "Shakespeare's Head"

Acknowledgments

I would like to thank all those who gave encouragement and made suggestions, especially Morri Creech, Philip Hoy, and Robert Schreur.

"Dickens on Fire" is indebted to Fred Kaplan's *Dickens: A Biography* for many matters of fact, occasional moments of phrasing, and a sense of the spirit of the man.

Contents

River of Song   15

1

Derecho   19
Stopping   20
Echolocation   21
Orogenesis   22
Autopoiesis   24
The Demon Dinanukht   25
Mark Strand   26
The End Was Over   27
Elegy for the American Sublime   29

2

Sometimes I Dream That I Am Not Walt Whitman   33
Let Them Say Whatever They Want   34
Returning to the Sea-shore   35
I Hear It Is Charged against Me   36
Like a Ghost I Returned   37
Some Tuesdays I Go to Lisbon   38
My Old Camerado, My Body   39

3

Runaway Blimp   43
Song of the NRA   46
Easter 2016   47
The Retreat   48

Contents

Coulrophobia with Line from Auden   50

4

Plein Air   53
The Ekphrastic Poet   54
Harvest Hobson   55
The Albatross   57
Giotto in Padua   58
Velázquez in Rome   59
Cézanne in Baltimore   60
The Compromised Ventriloquist   61

5

"My Sister Cut Me into Pieces"   67
"A Room of Zombies Smiled at Me"   68
"It's What's Inside Estranges Most"   69
"You'll Pay to Quote a Word of Mine"   70
"I Would Have Loathed Publicity"   71
"You Haven't Heard the End of Me"   72

6

Hardy's Writing Trousers   75
The Forsaken Singer   76
Aubade   77
Late Autumnal   78

Contents

Hobson's Choice 79
On Time 80
Shakespeare's Head 81

7

Dickens on Fire 89

A Note About the Author 99

Once, when he was a very old man, he came across a notebook he had kept as a boy, in which he had copied out poems by poets he particularly admired—Blake, Kipling, the early Yeats. His memory had now deteriorated to the point where he no longer recognized what these were, but mistook them for his own youthful compositions. He found himself in tears, surprised and delighted to discover, in his long forgotten juvenilia, such confidence, such skill, and such originality . . .

J. H. Hobson

A Human Touch: The Poetry of William Karl

River of Song

Who *said* that?
              Surfacing from sleep,
Seeing the curtains fringed with light,
I hear a music fading. Whose?
Part mine, part someone's. Cold and deep
The word-flow runs, and dark as night.

The dead keep singing. They don't sleep.
We wake, diminishing, and write.
I hear a music playing. Whose?
On runs the river, dark and deep
And cold as interstellar night.

1

Derecho

We didn't know the word, until it raced
Into the headlines, swamped the blogosphere,
    Shot tweets and postings, lightning-paced,
        From devastated scenes,
        And scrolled across our screens
    With "WARNING/FLASH FLOODS/STORMS/SEVERE"

As fast as when dark shelves of cloud arrive
Riding the gust front of a straight-line storm
    Huge downburst clusters swell and dive
        Unleashing hurricane-
        Force blasts of wind and rain,
    A squall line in bow echo form

With supercells and bookend vortices
Barrels for hours across hundreds of miles,
    Flips cars, flips trailers, jerks up trees,
        Peels roofs and levels walls,
        Grounds power poles and scrawls
    Its signature in rubbish piles

And strewn detritus all along its path
Of instantaneous destruction, cause
    To see some deity's hurled wrath
        In black skies and black rain,
        Some monster pleased by pain
    Batting our poor lives with its paws

Or pouncing down to rip the world askew
With one sharp thundrous cataclysmic blow,
    Crashing the lexicon. Right through.
        Wind-battered, water-blurred,
        We didn't know this word
    For "ruinous." But now we know.

Stopping

Whose woods these are we all know well
Though, tight-lipped, most refuse to tell,
Reluctant to assume the cost
Of any silly, childish spell

To make such hidden things stay lost:
No wind no ice no snow no frost,
No solid winter six feet deep
Nor'easter-swirled and bluster-tossed

Now blanketing a world asleep
Beneath the dark sky's starless sweep,
None of that. Just my double-take
To find, at my age, I still keep

Making my typical mistake,
Stopping beside this frozen lake
When I have promises to break
And miles to go before I wake.

Echolocation

Just as the bottlenose or pipistrelle
    Can map the world by sound
  With clicks and squeaks and high-pitched pings
    Emitted to rebound
    Through ocean or night air,
    Enabling them to tell
      Precisely where
    Tasty or nasty things
    Might swarm or swim or lurk
  In thick dark or in liquid murk,
Using cochlear adaptation
    As fine-tuned instrument
For foraging and navigation
    In lieu of sight or scent,

So this tries, as it sings both high and low,
    Flicking in fricatives
And whispering in sibilants,
    To bounce back off what gives
    A rising assonance
    To every rounded "o,"
      A resonance
    Echoing those first chants
    Projecting songs to come
In fine-tuning the medium
To double, treble, crest, and flow
    With "sun," " moon," "morning star,"
Like flocks of leaves, by which we know
    Exactly where we are.

Orogenesis

When moonstruck spirits said
To William Butler Yeats,
"We've come to give you metaphors
For poetry," this isn't what they meant:
An upward buckling of tectonic plates
That elevated ocean floors,
One hell-raising Devonian event
Whose record can be read

In long striated strips
Of orogenic belts,
In seashells found on mountaintops
And smooth granitic batholiths. On shifts
Of molten tides the crust thickens or melts,
The viscous circle never stops,
The roaring river spits and splits and lifts,
The mantle, sliding, slips

So quakes and tremors scar
Our psyches and our lands,
For any pretty hillside town
Built near a jagged fault, even with care
And solid stuff, by practiced, steady hands,
Can in a flash come crashing down
As tragic cries inflect the dust-filled air
And landscape stands ajar.

Nothing is stable, static.
Surface is always flow.
Structures of posed placidity,
The chiseled symmetries of form, conceal
Compressed volcanic agony below,
Intemperate liquidity
Whose outbursts, unpredictable, reveal
A flare for the dramatic

Orogenesis

    Ambition to ascend.
    Thrust by deforming thrust
  The fresh material extrudes,
And year by year the Himalayas rise,
Mounting colliding continental crust
    At clear breath-taking altitudes
To redefine the precinct of the skies
      From which the clouds depend.

    Not even mountains last
    Forever, but when all
  Is said they last a good long time.
"Not marble nor the gilded monuments"
Sustain comparison with what we'll call
    The geological sublime,
Or what is, gauged by proper instruments,
      New, and coming up fast.

Autopoiesis

Some truths it might be shrewder *not* to tell.
Take the example of the single cell,
Eukaryotic, compartmentalized,
From man, or plant, or mold, however sized,
With membrane, nucleus, and organelles.
The self-maintaining chemistry of cells
Renders a thing intact, autonomous,
Whether alone, or deep inside of us,
So organized that every transformation
Becomes another act of self-creation,
A unity of network, a machine
That allocates each acid and protein
Its proper role and place inside the whole
That is itself its proper place and role.
As Maturana and Varela saw,
The neat dynamic of this inner law
Offers a polymorphous metaphor
Adaptable to what we want it for,
To systems theory, sociology,
Or literary studies. Poetry
Accommodates such figuring of what
Is not unlike a couplet snapping shut,
Leaving us outside. What we set in play
Insists on having its peculiar say
To spin the world it shapes, inscribed, compact,
The heartless, self-affirming artifact
Whose firework canopy and diamond show
Tell us the truth lies where we'd best not go.
Marking the interface of sound and sense,
The poem is its own intelligence
Out there alone and making making do.
It doesn't need me, reader, or need you.

The Demon Dinanukht

Sunk in his chair, he seems half man, half book,
Inhabiting both worlds, reading himself
To sleep beside his drink, though he may lie
About falling asleep, half man half book,
And even lie about reading, himself.

And you have felt, yourself, half man, half book,
Felt someone else entirely, reading himself
Right through you, past you, riffs of sea and sky
Turning the ruffled page, half man half book
Drifting between blue worlds, reading himself.

The demon Dinanukht, half man, half book,
Idles between the worlds, reading himself.
Lifetimes he turns his pages, seated by
The waters clear as glass, half man half book
Perfecting his reflection, reading himself.

And Old John Wallace seemed half man half book
Turning to winter air, reading himself
Accumulating in slow drifts of sky,
Old man, old massive head, half man, half book,
Half dying star, half starlight, reading himself.

Mark Strand

When I came to the end of the dream, there was Mark Strand.
We were in a vast hall, where the ceiling was too high to see,
And the light slanted down from above, and a cold wind blew.
We sat on a bench in the back. A little ways off,
A teacher was teaching a class, and she asked him to speak,
But he shook his head: he was too tired. Then he turned
To me, and he said, "I don't write anymore. I don't
Even look at the moon. But I read." Then he smiled. "When you read
The books you most love for the last time, you see
The great works of imagination get better and better.
When you come to that passage where, arrayed in battalions,
With all their flashing armor and flapping banners
And bright wings fanning the starlight, the heavenly host
Throws down its spears, you wonder, although you've read it
A hundred times, 'Will it really happen again?',
And when it does, you are surprised." There were tears
In his eyes as he said this. But were they tears of sadness,
Or tears of joy, or were they just caused by the wind,
That cold wind blowing and blowing? Then he was gone,
And the teacher was gone, with her class, and the students' voices,
And all I could hear in the hall was the sound of the wind.

The End Was Over

The end was over, over long ago.
If others survived in isolated places
Beyond the horizon, we had no way to know.

No one remembered names, or styles, or faces.
Perhaps some thoughts occurred, but no one spoke.
If travelers passed by, they left no traces.

Were someone to tell a story or a joke
No one would even begin to understand.
If someone walked out on the ice, it broke.

Things happened or didn't happen. Nothing was planned.
We moved more slowly when we tried to hurry.
It hindered us if someone lent a hand.

What little we could see was always blurry.
All we could hear was silence everywhere.
Perhaps we should have worried. We didn't worry.

Perhaps we should have cared. We didn't care
Enough to leave those will-numbing confines,
All vacancy and stillness and cold air,

Where signs meant nothing. Not that there were signs.
There was no central point from which to see
The emptiness keep forming empty lines

That led us back to us. And who were "we"?
There was no "we" left. Everyone was gone.
The only person left was only me.

The End Was Over

In that white world I was myself alone
The figure of a man against the snow.
The wind droned on, unending, monotone.

I liked it there. But that was long ago.

Elegy for the American Sublime

And what, in the end, can the solitary man
Make of the landscape he's projected by?
A few dead leaves, the puny, denuded trees,
The emptiness filling up with nothing at all?

The annals of the American sublime
Shrink to a handful of names, then forget the names.
The sun comes up on a terrified new world
Stripped of its rich, protective coverings,

Its canopies, its finial adjectives,
Its columned boreal abundancies,
Its tropical imbrications of this and that.
The ice shelves crack and calve into the seas.

Across the wide waste a solitary bird
Flies straight through the center of absence, then flies on.
The thought of a palm tree never crosses its mind.
It navigates mnemonic indices

Although the world it remembers no longer exists,
The wetlands no longer exist, Key West is long gone.
If it lands, it will imagine an audience
Imagining a song. Then it will sing.

2

Sometimes I Dream That I Am Not Walt Whitman

Sometimes I dream that I am not Walt Whitman,
That I am an engineer, or an airplane pilot,
Or a schoolteacher, or a soldier, or a traveling salesman,
Not a poet living his afterlife through his poems.

I enjoy those dreams. I enjoy waking to find they were only dreams.

Let Them Say Whatever They Want

Let them say whatever they want about me on the Internet,
I am fine with it. I am all for communication in an instant.

I like the Internet, but sometimes it makes me feel like an old man.
Then I remember: I am only one hundred and ninety-nine.

Returning to the Sea-shore

Returning to the sea-shore after more than a century
I dally my feet in the waves as I did when a boy,
I see the developments, the condominia, then I do not see them at all,
Just the marsh grass and the cattails covering the dunes,
The long, low clouds and the dark rolling shroud of the sea.

I Hear It Is Charged against Me

I hear it is charged against me that I have become an institution,
A monument, a study, an industry,
With biographers and bibliographers and editorial apparatuses.

In my lifetime I didn't much care about institutions,
And now in my afterlife I care even less.
Whatever they say I am, you can be certain I'm not.

Please desist with your commentaries and annotations, however
 well intended,
For they are completely beside the point, and always will be.
Go walk in the fields and woods, go walk by the sea at night and
 look up at the stars.

See what I mean? Yes, now you see what I mean.

Like a Ghost I Returned

Like a ghost I returned to my old house in Camden
And tagged along with a tour group, listening to the guide
Recite details of my life there, some of them true.

I saw, one more time, the room where I slept and wrote
(They had my old pen on display, I could almost reach out and
 touch it),
The room where I sat with guests, the kitchen where Mary cooked
 for me,
The room where they laid out my corpse and a thousand people
 filed past.

Who would have thought I had so many friends and admirers?
And what did they think they would see? It was just a corpse.
The real me had moved on, living and breathing in poems.

I am no staid collection of facts and artifacts.

I am the waves in the seas of grass, I am the wind in the leaves.

Some Tuesdays I Go to Lisbon

Some Tuesdays I go to Lisbon to see my friend Álvaro de Campos.
We walk down to the docks and watch the boats come in,
Or stroll up the Rua do Ouro, or visit his favorite tobacco shop,
All the time talking about what's real and what isn't.

He imagines I have serenity, and envies me for it.
But I am not serene, even now that I'm posthumous,
And I certainly wasn't serene when I had a body,
Just accepting of everything.

I try to explain the difference, but he can't quite hear it.

He thinks he is nothing (he isn't), and savors his misery, his boredom.
I suspect it depresses him that he was never a person,
That he only lived in poems, and in peoples' minds,
But I only live in poems, and in peoples' minds,
So there is less difference between us than there would be if he
    were human.

I guess it cheers him up when I point this out, but I can't really tell.
One minute he's moping, the next minute he's running in circles,
    shouting ecstatically.

He always asks me to stay a few days, or a week.
But on Wednesdays I go to Chile, to see Pablo Neruda.

My Old Camerado, My Body

My old camerado, my body, how long has it been?

You from whom I was indivisible, to whom I adhered,
One with me, one with the best of me, the best part of me, all of me,
You whose sensations would dazzle and overwhelm me
Until all my thoughts were electric and nothing but,
Diminished, over the years, to a slight tingling,
Then to only the ghost of a tingling,
The memory of a memory of a memory.

Today I'm not sure I would recognize my own face.

There is, I admit, a peace of sorts in cessation,
A release from desire, from desire's waiting and hoping.
I suppose I should be grateful, but I don't feel grateful.
I am the poet of the body who has no body.
Nobody tallies that loss more surely than I do
As I sing one last song for you, my old camerado, my body.

3

Runaway Blimp

On daily walks I'd seen
It shimmer in the eastern sky,
Glossed with an eerily synthetic sheen
Early morning light would intensify,
Afloat like an air-borne precipitate
Hanging, ethereal and argentine,
By its bright, identical mate
High above Aberdeen,

On trial, when inflated
And raised, as JLENS, or Joint Land
Attack Cruise Missile Defense Elevated
Netted Sensor System, part of a planned
Upgrade of East Coast aerial surveillance
Whose virtues, prematurely celebrated
For scope, precision, instant valence,
Proved much exaggerated:

The blimp struggled to track
Objects in flight, discriminate
Our friendly stuff from stuff that might attack,
Or quickly, properly communicate
With all the crisscrossed elements of air
Defense, bumping its "activation" back
For yet more tweaking and repair,
Drawing Congressional flak

As costs ballooned, and it
Was tagged a "zombie program," loss
Piled high on loss (deterring not a whit
Its advocate, General James E. "Hoss"
Cartwright, who fought to keep it, then signed on
After retirement, as lax rules permit,
To serve its maker, Raytheon,
For handsome benefit),

Runaway Blimp

    Symbolic of the bloated
    Unindustrious complex, bought
And sold, the useless, shamelessly promoted
Gadgets unneeded in the wars unfought,
As representatives who know the score
Protect the massive boondoggles they floated
    And, past the fast revolving door,
        Get paid for how they voted;

    And now, as if to make
    A show of excess run amok
And prove its project one big fat mistake,
A multi-billion dollar clusterfuck,
Taking advantage of some windy weather
The blimp has wriggled loose and made a break,
    Dragging its mile-long Kevlar tether
        In its destructive wake,

    Sans clue or caveat,
    For random parts unknown, gone rogue
While flummoxed handlers wonder where it's at,
Turned star, meme-of-the-moment, Twitter vogue,
When scattered residents happen to spy
("O Amos, gookamoedoe!" "What is *that*?"),
    Lurching across the autumn sky,
        The errant aerostat

    Which can't self-disenable
    (The fail-safe mechanism failed
Once the unstable ship got too unstable)
To stop percussive impacts now entailed
As side effects of blimpomania,
As right through power line and fence and stable
    For swaths of Pennsylvania
        Swings of its massive cable

Runaway Blimp

    Slice arbitrarily,
  Careening off like pumped-up teens
On a joyride, intoxicated, free,
Though now tracked by two scrambled F-16s,
And when state troopers, sent to do it in
Once it descends and gets snagged on a tree,
    Pepper its self-repairing skin
      With shotguns, finally

    It shrivels back to land,
  Downed in Moreland Township, PA,
And soon they'll want to know at High Command
Why some fool things just up and run away,
Like love, or metaphor, or public debt, so
Bigwigs and pointy-heads might understand
    How such a costly craft could get so
      Completely out of hand.

Song of the NRA

"Guns don't kill people, people do,"
People with guns. Our native right
To stroll forth armed for mortal fight
Will stand its ground. It might kill you,
It might kill me, or anyone.
America I've got my gun!

A firearm doesn't pull the trigger
Each time a toddler shoots a parent.
We need more rifles, that's apparent,
Sleek, rapid-fire, and better, bigger.
There's one that's right for everyone.
America I've got my gun!

In bars, in churches, parks and schools
We'd best be armed. If they attack
We'll whip our guns out and fight back.
We'll shoot it out like bloody fools
While people scream and duck and run.
America I've got my gun!

Murder might as well be mass.
Register the numbers slain
At a movie, on a train,
Little children in a class,
People dancing, having fun . . .
America I've got my gun!

Orlando, Blacksburg, Columbine,
Newtown, Charleston, San Ysidro,
Aurora, and San Bernardino . . .
But Congress better toe the line
Or someone to their right will run.
Just watch yourself. I've got my gun.

Easter 2016

Hatred and fear surge on the bitter winds.
New ignorance gives credence to each lie,
The demagogue echoes the roiling cry.
Our common sense of purpose, whipsawed, bends
And starts to splinter. Urged by the angry storm,
Worst things worsen. The body politic
Gnaws its own innards, retches, grows more sick.
The harmed are drawn to what would do more harm.

Target the other, blame it all on Them
And down we go, shot by the messenger.
Such ugly means mean even uglier ends
Would body-slam the hapless passenger.
Hatred and fear surge on the bitter winds.
Dark hour. Rough beast. The slouch towards Bethlehem.

The Retreat

after Hugo

It snowed. Now, self-defeated by conquest,
For the first time the eagle had failed a test.
Dark days! Slowly the emperor returned.
Behind his back, Moscow still smoked and burned.
It snowed. From winter's avalanche of pain
After each white plain rose another white plain.
One couldn't make out companies or flags.
A great army turned a herd of scraps and rags.
No one could tell the center from the flanks.
It snowed. The wounded sheltered against the flanks
Of frozen horses; sentinels were ghosts;
The silent buglers, frigid at their posts,
Sat rigid in their saddles, dusted with snow,
Lips fastened to the horns they could not blow.
Grape-shot and musket-balls, mixed with snow-flakes,
Kept raining; shivering, pondering mistakes,
Grenadiers wandered, mustaches caked with ice.
It snowed, it always snowed. Wind gripped like a vice.
Soldiers, marching, slipped on ground glazed with frost,
Stumbling, barefoot and starving, utterly lost.
The men of war, no heart left to fight back,
Shadows against the dark sky, black on black,
Filed through the mist like dreams of misery.
Pure solitude, huge, horrible to see,
Surrounded them in silent retribution.
The snow kept up its quiet contribution,
A great white shroud blanketing the whole force.
The doomed knew they would die, alone of course.
How to escape the country's double curse?
Two foes: the tsar, the north. The north was worse.
They scrapped the cannons; the carriages were used
For firewood. Those who lay down died. Confused,
Dejected, they kept retreating. The white waste
Consumed them. One whole regiment was erased
While sleeping, buried by folds of snow, undone

The Retreat

As pulverized by Hannibal or the Hun.
Wagons and stretchers, the wounded, the half-dead
Jammed bridges, crushed together as they fled.
Ten thousand fell asleep, one hundred woke.
Ney, who once moved an army when he spoke,
Squabbled over his watch with three Cossacks.
Each night the alarm would sound. Then the attacks.
The spectral soldiers grabbed their guns, surrounded
By a rushing, terrifying blur that sounded
Like shrieking vultures, circling, striking again,
Appalling squadrons, whirlwinds of wild men.
An army was destroyed in one dark night.
Still the emperor lingered, watching their flight,
As a giant oak tree, subject to the axe
When calamity, the cutter, scales and attacks
Its grandeur, though still standing and still tall,
Shudders watching its lopped-off branches fall.
Commanders and soldiers died, each in their turn.
A remaining few believers could discern,
Huddling in devotion around his tent,
How his shadow on the canvas came and went.
Not knowing what to think, quailed, stupefied,
The emperor turned to God; his glorious pride
Trembled. Seeing his legions scattered about
Dead and dying, Napoleon cried out
(Presuming the destined settling of some score),
"Is this my punishment, great God of War?"
And then he heard, out of the shadows and snow,
A voice pronounce his name, and answer: "No."

Coulrophobia with Line from Auden

Each day we're pummeled by the news.
The morning's storm of nasty tweets
Gathers a pool of exegetes.
The President's in golfing shoes.

Whipped commentators commentate
Upon a world flipped upside down.
Sad props to our commanding clown
Collapse in a reeling crisis state

Out of control he isn't in.
Tools the lobbies brought and sold
Open a fake news Age of Gold.
The public takes it, on the chin.

Meanwhile more vulnerable, vast
Networks of ecosystem start
To melt and dry and break apart,
Silently and very fast.

4

Plein Air

What *is* this landscape, rising like a dream
Through somnolent evasions of the mind?
A bay, some boats, a sand bar, a blue sky,
The bluest sky, clear water, aquamarine,
Two green peninsular hills to frame the scene,
The boats becalmed or anchored, and, far out,
A steamer stuck all silent afternoon,
The only agitation dips and swerves
Of frigate birds and pelicans and gulls . . .

It might be Martinique, or Guadeloupe,
Or Dominica, or some other isle.
It might be paradise, it might be real—
The world we dream on when we dream the world
Is picture perfect, and we're outside time
Or time has grown so large there is no time
Or all the time in the world to linger here
Where palm tree fronds apportion zones of shade,
To sip the essences of sea and sky
Like some exotic drink, and feel, just now,
The tiniest intentions of a breeze.

And we know it was never always this way
And ever will be, the two of us, alone
Together in the sunshot world blended
By memory, until the light declines
And all we loved to look on dims, obscured,
And sign by sign the alien stars arise.

The Ekphrastic Poet

The ekphrastic poet seeks a fine vignette
For the conjunction of the sister arts.
He looks and looks. He hasn't found it yet.

He wants a scene too vivid to forget,
A whole composed of quintessential parts
An ekphrastic poet needs for his vignette:

A still life, maybe, wineglass with baguette,
Or rustic view, with oxen pulling carts.
He looks, and looks. He hasn't found it, yet

Believes in it. He hardly feels regret
For all the botched approaches, the false starts.
The ekphrastic poet sees his first vignette

Will take more looking. Arranging his *palette*
In imitation of the color charts,
He looks as if he hasn't found it yet.

When the spectrum forms a secret alphabet,
When words turn pictures, or when spades turn hearts,
The ekphrastic poet seizes his vignette.
For now, he looks. He hasn't found it. Yet.

Harvest Hobson

He was a poet, but the poets who garnered praise
And paraded about admired by everyone
Were ones he despised (no wit, no irony,
Faux-philosophical pretentiousness),
And most of all he hated Harvest Hobson,
A poet who wasn't nearly as good as himself.

He decided to take the whole gang on himself,
Composing a panegyric of mock praise
In the form of a scathing essay on Harvest Hobson
For a publication read by everyone,
"Harvest Hobson and the New Pretentiousness,"
A wicked assault of withering irony.

But no one seemed to get the irony.
They came away believing he himself
Was a fan of what he called "Pretentiousness,"
Thought it a noble thing, deserving praise,
And that he really felt, like everyone,
Nothing but admiration for Harvest Hobson.

His essay helped secure, for Harvest Hobson,
A major prize. The bitterest irony
Was suddenly to be seen by everyone
As the champion of Hobson, who thanked him himself,
To be known, now, as a critic, and receive praise
As the bold advocate of Pretentiousness.

He authored a screed against Pretentiousness,
Viciously ridiculing Harvest Hobson
As a poet unworthy of notice, much less praise,
Without the slightest hint of irony.
From the moment it appeared, he found himself
Cursed, hated, and insulted by everyone,

Harvest Hobson

His talks and readings canceled, every one,
A snake whose treacherous pretentiousness
Had led him, desperate to promote himself,
To attack his benefactor, Harvest Hobson,
To whom he had once bent even his iron knee.
He grew confused, unable to appraise

A poem, or tell himself from Harvest Hobson.
They were one and the same. Perhaps pretentiousness
Was better than irony, and worthy of praise.

The Albatross

after Baudelaire

Often, to amuse themselves, the sailors seize
What shadows their ship as it glides along its way,
The albatross, high lord of the gulfs and seas,
Their indolent companion turned their prey.

Hobbled on shipboard, baffled, the sky king's
Deposed, a joke his dignity abhors.
Clumsy, ashamed, he feels his huge white wings
Drag at his sides, useless as unmanned oars.

This soaring voyager, how awkward and weak,
How comical, tormented by the crew!
One torturer sticks a cutty in his beak;
Limping, one mimics the cripple who once flew.

The poet, like this rider of the skies,
Wandered the trade winds, laughing at earth-bound things,
But grounded where people hoot and criticize
Can't walk, encumbered by his outsized wings.

Giotto in Padua

Arena Chapel

A blue so blue it seems the radiant day
Has entered the room without the glittering
Sunlight, so deep, so soft the flittering
Angels look real as birds as they loop away

Above these curves of rediscovered mass,
Delineated body taking form
Beneath those robes (ground: flatness was the norm),
Fresco by fresco, here. It came to pass:

Clear narrative with spare embellishment,
Space structured to give character its feeling
(Faux marble frieze, faux chamber, vaulted ceiling),
And dazzling emissaries, heaven-sent . . .

Van Eyck stood right here, Leonardo, too,
Titian and Rubens, Turner, Klee, and Proust
Took tracings for eventual *mots justes*
Washed in this essence, this original blue.

Velázquez in Rome

Galleria Doria Pamphilj

Dispatched to Italy from the Spanish court
To purchase high art of whatever sort
(Statuary, Veronese, Titian),
The man Velázquez accepted a commission
To paint that tough, embittered misanthrope,
The hardly innocent Pamphilj pope,
Driven to place his own grim, taut complexion
Amid the measureless wealth of his collection:
The Laocoön, Apollo Belvedere,
The Stefaneschi Polyptych, the sheer
Heaven of Stanza della Segnatura,
Plus oddities, a camera obscura,
Murals of courtiers with platyrrhini....
Worn out from battles with the Barberini
And flexing the power of the Holy See
To quash the rising Jansenist heresy,
The weary pontiff caught himself reflected
In wariness, arrested and perfected
(Reynolds called it "the finest picture in Rome":
Velázquez carefully took a copy home)
By *manera abreviada*, bold
And vital, mirroring each textured fold
In pinpoint lines, with no soft touch to flatter
The human subject, flawed heart of the matter,
Though subtleties of velvet, linen, silk,
Rich reds and creamy whites (like blood, like milk)
Impart a dignity, if not a grace,
To the shrewd force contracted in that face
Whose owner, seen so clearly, and seen through,
Said only, "*troppo vero*": it is too true.

Cézanne in Baltimore

Mont Sainte-Victoire Seen from the Bibémus Quarry
Cone Collection, Baltimore Museum of Art

He painted it, then painted it again
For twenty years or more, week after week
Layering slope, ridge, double limestone peak,
Till rhomboid, trapezoid, block and plane,
Green pines, deep orange cliffs, mauve-tinted sky
Composed an art that's somehow both abstract
And representational: when we react
With five steps back to realign the eye

Space opens in a rush of vertigo
Between the near trees and the quarry wall,
Perspective drops this room, which seemed so small,
Echoing into cavernous effects.
Mont Sainte-Victoire still towers over Aix
Both on and off the canvas. Scene from below.

The Compromised Ventriloquist

1

Gastromancy, vibration in the gut
    Tuned to the presence of the dead,
Possessed the medium to utter what,
    Digested, triggered hope or dread

In questioners delighted or aghast
    At all they thought they finally knew.
To tell the future or reveal the past
    Was dangerous. The darkest clue

Doomed sacrificial youths and beasts.
    Dim ravings, guttural, abrupt,
Translated to hexameters by priests
    In versions polished and corrupt

Proved riddles no less difficult to crack.
    The truth was rarely clear or kind.
Cautious Lysander wound up stabbed in the back,
    Croesus conquered, Oedipus blind.

The Compromised Ventriloquist

2

What once was supernatural decree
    Became, in time, a party trick
Crowds at the music halls would pay to see.
    The animated dumb sidekick,

Charlie McCarthy, Sailor Jim, or Coster Joe,
    Though just a cheeky, wiseass puppet,
Would show his straight man up throughout the show,
    Flip every quibble and one up it.

Oracular enshrinement? Oh so past.
    Ventriloquy was entertainment.
Magic was stagecraft, voice the artful cast.
    Nobody wondered what the strain meant.

3

Nearing the scribbled end, he took the stage,
    The compromised ventriloquist,
His bare-bones theater the haunted page.
    Obscurity, "uncouthe unkiste,"

Held no protection from the talking dead.
    No charm or curse could exorcise
The choir of sirens singing in his head
    Inspiring another exercise.

His "own distinctive style" at last? Dream on.
    Some stuff he made up, sure. But then
Those ghostly demarcations would stream on
    Flooding his studio again

To wash him up and out and down the drain.
    Too influential, they impressed
And he was pressed. But why complain
    About not being self-possessed?

Conspiring to imprison him for years,
    Through harmony and ornament
The arch conductors of the crystal spheres
    Abused him as their instrument.

Black magic? Maybe. Cheating? Well, that too.
    Who's talking? Uh oh. Hold the phone.
He was the dummy they kept speaking through
    In words that were and weren't his own.

5

"My Sister Cut Me into Pieces"

My sister cut me into pieces
    As soon as I was dead.
Worlds upon worlds I'd organized
    She'd organize instead.

My lines grew titles, sprouted rhymes,
    Gained period and "sense,"
And all my artful books were strewn
    By clueless negligence.

And when a man stitched up my leaves,
    With microscopic eye
Aligning all my holes and stains
    Right where they used to lie,

Just as my long-lost reassembled
    Lineaments shone through,
Forgetting all his labor's love
    He rearranged me, too.

"A Room of Zombies Smiled at Me"

A room of zombies smiled at me
    And offered me a chair,
So I sat down with them. We waited,
    Nowhere and everywhere,

And waited, listening to time,
    Alert though we were dead.
Who were those rapt initiates
    Repeating all we'd said?

"It's What's Inside Estranges Most"

It's what's inside estranges most.
    The landscape of the moon
Would seem just as familiar as
    Our favorite childhood tune

Compared to the immense reserve
    That opens in the mind
Dimensions we can't comprehend.
    Our terms recede behind

Where solitude turns company,
    Where agony seems numb,
When caution triggers recklessness,
    Intelligence stays dumb,

And every burning nerve we have
    Goes marble, petrified,
And we cease half-believing in
    A different world outside.

Out there, back then, in space and time,
    There's something with my name.
People will hear things differently.
    The words sing just the same.

"You'll Pay to Quote a Word of Mine"

You'll pay to quote a word of mine.
    The "Dickinson estate"
Returns a profit every line,
    Protectors at the gate

Whose racket is protecting me
    So I can't get to you.
Sister, reader, friend, ephebe,
    The thieves won't let me through!

"I Would Have Loathed Publicity"

I would have loathed publicity
    For my most private hopes.
My jottings and imaginings
    On scraps of envelopes

Were never meant to be displayed
    Where anyone could look,
All reproduced on pages of
    A coffee-table book.

But homely, careful, practical
    Economy supplies
An industry of scholarship
    Nothings to fetishize.

What seizure isn't violation?
    What serifed theft not crime?
But Sappho, too, in bits and shards,
    Made her hard way through time

Till every little shred of her,
    Canonical and vast,
Got spread out case by case in The
    Museum of the Past,

Each elemental letter now
    Made flesh, incarnadine,
And she a force field in herself.
    The future is all mine.

"You Haven't Heard the End of Me"

You haven't heard the end of me
    By war nor flood nor fire.
I'll take the tops of heads right off,
    I'll twist each nerve to wire

Attuned so waves of sound erode
    The boundaries of sense
And swamp or just obliterate
    All tattered evidence

Of everything you thought you knew
    The simplest thing about,
And consciousness is ocean now,
    And you keep drifting out

Where sea is one big heaving bowl
    And sky its massive twin,
And rising to the wind and waves
    I differ to begin.

So grammar, logic, rhetoric
    Like constellations fall
As I keep figuring – beyond
    Horizon, beyond all.

6

Hardy's Writing Trousers

Where are the hounds who ran the land,
    The Chowders and the Bowsers
    Who bayed at everything,
Or rumbled in a dust-storm of a band
    Swerving right or wrong as
Led by the zig-zag skitters of their prey?
       They had their day.
    They did not last as long as
The piece of raveled, triple-knotted string
That held up Thomas Hardy's writing trousers.

Where are the folk who owned the land,
    The holiday carousers
    Who played at the latest thing,
Whirling together as the village band
    Wound up a final song as
Shalloon and sash and kerchief caught the sway?
       They had their day.
    They did not last as long as
The piece of raveled, triple-knotted string
That held up Thomas Hardy's writing trousers.

Where are the old ones knew the land,
    The forkers, diggers, dowsers
    Who stayed at some hard thing
While fields closed in and pass-through routes were banned,
    With wand and spade and prong as
Busy as if their way were the only way?
       They had their day.
    They did not last as long as
The piece of raveled, triple-knotted string
That held up Thomas Hardy's writing trousers.

The Forsaken Singer

ACS

When his music defined what the young folk wanted,
When to sing so purely was risky and brave,
And his drop-dead artistry, echo-haunted
By concatenations of wind and wave
Where the foam flower blooms and the sea mew hovers,
Made the high tide fill the most secretive nooks
With studied perfection, true poetry lovers
      Bought his books.

He sang as if there were no tomorrows,
As if past and present were one fluid tense
Full of tacit longings and private sorrows,
As if beauty were meaning and sound were sense.
And all those who heard him were certain they knew
Why he sang as he sang, for a darkling change
Swept over the seascape to render their view
      Rich and strange.

But fashion, as fashioned, falls victim to time.
The polished, percussive extremes of a style
Swirling in arabesque rhythm and rhyme
For a while seemed just right. But just for a while.
What the past most admired the future forecloses.
When the sea winds rise and the sea pines sway
Some things get, like summer's most delicate roses,
      Blown away.

Oh yes he was king of the cats, whose fame
Seemed permanent, scripted by stars. And yet
How many, today, remember his name?
The world doesn't end, but we do forget.
A singer falls silent a hundred years.
Rare bookstores vanish. Small libraries close.
What happens to music when no one hears?
      No one knows.

Aubade

Recall your gift, my love. Recall
What I so longed for in my youth.
I wanted beauty, thought it truth.
I wanted love, and thought it all.

I thought the ecstasies of song
Whispering immortality
Would ransom me and rescue me
From my old anguish. I was wrong.

But, beautiful, your sunrise steals
In flakes of fire far up the sky.
I tell myself my mourning lie:
Your shining tears, your silver wheels.

Late Autumnal

Peace. Mists. The sense of something near its end.
Last fruits have fallen, leaves have fallen, too.
Harvest was plumpness, sweetness, swell and bend,
Full-bodied. But that's done. The bees are through.
Winnowing, gleaning, reaping—all are past.
What could be saved has been saved. Now in store
Just coldness, hardness, frost. A light wind dies.
We had enough, and then some. We wanted more
From this, our perfect season which couldn't last.
The stubble darkens. Days are fading fast.
A final swallow, twittering. The skies.

Hobson's Choice

What needs old Hobson for his broken bones
And girt, his sloughed-off skin? Shifter at last,
Supt on, a ghost of motion, pulled by worms,
No coupled, hobbled load of final terms
Carried too far and stacked like "pilèd stones"
Adds one more breath. Time numbers. Motion past,

He turns up in a phrase, a paradox
Shrewdly maneuvered, weighted, offering
A choice of one, the horse nearest the door
Or none at all. *His* terms, pressed through threescore-
Plus years of riding out a thousand shocks,
Stand witness to his name, though angels sing.

On Time

Slow, previous time: with every year your pace
Accelerates, as weeks speed past like hours
Plummeting into darkness and dead space,
Till mind forgets the body's slackened powers.
Each season flips its scenes of sun and rain
      To race aslant across
      Our little field of loss
      And come and go again.
The pleasures the once greedy self consumed
As individual now blur, entombed
In riddled memory; even that kiss
      That seemed the point of bliss,
When two good hearts conjoined for mutual good,
Turns joyless, taken by the darkening flood:
      Our past, dead on the line.
You, signified, present your form. We sign.
      Contracted, monotone,
What makes us happy? Sight, and sight alone,
But less and less. The constellations climb
    The winter sky, and will not quit.
We're tired of stars, the flashing whole of it.
We miss gross earth. And flesh. And chance. And thee o time.

Shakespeare's Head

"That skull had a tongue in it, and could sing once."

1

GOOD FREND FOR IESVS SAKE FORBEARE,
TO DIGG THE DVST ENCLOASED HEARE:
BLESE BE Y̆ MAN Y̆ SPARES THES STONES,
AND CVRST BE HE Y̆ MOVES MY BONES.

And cursed be sexton, parish clerk,
Or any man whose dirty work
Disturbs my poor dust where it lies.
I'll see you, though through other eyes.

The dead know how to set things right
Ghosting the corners of the night,
To find and leave you cold in bed,
Your imperfections on your head.

My blessing may do little good
To those refraining as they should,
But if you thrive by doing ill
My curse will mark you, yes it will.

2

> But how to reconcile
> The poet of such agony and lust,
> Of worldliness, rhetorical bravura,
> And infinite variety of style,
>> And wit, and *sprezzatura*,
>> With this insipid bust

Of bluish Cotswold limestone, set in its niche?
"A self-satisfied pork butcher" (Dover
    Wilson), quill pen in hand,
He looks thick-headed, ordinary, rich.
    Whole worlds at his command?
    The cloud-capp'd show was over.

Fears of the charnel house, of disinterred
Confusion, ossuary mix and match.
    Who's knocked about the mazard,
Chopless? Well, anyone. Without a word
    Poor luck finds out the hazard,
    Some clay a hole to patch.

    Here lies. Commemorate,
Like any other man, the matchless bard.
Like golden lads and girls. The final stage.
"Stay passenger." Regard the name, the date.
    Trust to the living page,
    And pray. The rest is hard.

Shakespeare's Head

3

All your precautions can't anticipate
The odd macabre fads of future days:
The burgeoning celebrity skull craze
That led collectors to decapitate

Beethoven, Haydn, Swift, Sir Thomas Browne,
Geronimo and Goya and de Sade,
Led someone to pry up your stone, then prod
Your resting spot to find you, three feet down,

Shrouded not coffined, and detach their prize.
Ground penetrating radar (GPR)
Discovers you're not where we think you are,
At least your skull is not. To our surprise,

An odd disturbance where your head should be
("A strange brick structure"—what's *that* doing there?)
Suggests an infiltration and repair.
Custodians of Holy Trinity

Won't give permission for an excavation.
With or without your head, they'll let you lie. . . .
Cue the hideous lines, the shriek owl cry,
The sheeted dead of Gothic machination

Who squeak and gibber, cue men all in fire
Walking the streets like portents, dews of blood,
These late eclipses, wing to th' rooky wood,
Burst cerements. Lights up. Bare ruined choir.

4

Curse or plea, it matters not.
Greedy finds so Greedy takes,
Scripts the coda, all mistakes.
Mutilation of the plot

Turns romance to tragic farce,
Mocks the poet's dying wish,
Serves his head as on a dish.
Mystery we'll never parse,

Clueless, bootless as the dead.
Property appalled, the self
Reams of paper on a shelf,
Beauty, truth, and all that fled.

Harbinger come far too near,
Invitation in a curse.
Hard, now, to imagine worse.
Like the snows of yesteryear

Constancy is for the birds.
Greedy takes what Greedy finds,
Casts it to the viewless winds.
All's defunctive. Blot these words.

5

Foul deeds will rise. The heart with strings of steel
Will bow before the altar, flush with guilt.
Confess your sins, though none will be forgiven,
Not heinous theft, nor murderous intent,
Nor profit from imaginary crime.
A magpie's not a man, though black and white,
Blackness of heart, the white of cowardice
Strutting in borrowed feathers, cap-a-pie.
It's better to be vile and vile esteemed
Than not to be, however rank your crimes.

Ladies and gentlemen, *I* stole Shakespeare's head.
At some point in the past, I won't say how
—Strings pulled, palms greased, equipment commandeered—
Jump at the dark-shoaled middle of the night
I slipped past lime trees, found an open door,
By candlelight crowbarred his ledger stone,
Jabbed my right hand right through his threadbare shroud,
Fingered vermicular dust to find his skull
Then gripped it through the eye sockets and took it.
It's sitting on my desk, watching me now.

7

Dickens on Fire

Precipitate, determined, absolute
In bending all around him to his will,
    Inflammable and volatile
        And furiously driven,
    Prone to pity and self-pity,
        Oblivious yet acute,
Cruel to his wife, kind to the destitute,
        A man of style
           And skill
    And fueled propensity
    To slog on mile by soggy mile
    Crackling with charged intensity,
        And all the while
Keen eyes fixed on the goals toward which he'd striven,
Fame and its fortunes, charity, Gad's Hill,

Dickens was steadied, somewhat, by routine
Keeping his reckless energy on track,
    A morning shower, quick, ice-cold,
        Then breakfast, then ascending
    To wrestle at his writing desk
        With how to set the scene
For tension, sentiment, an unforeseen
        And manifold
           Attack
    Of twists and turns, grotesque
    Incinerations, crimes of old,
    Kind quirks that verge on the burlesque
        Just as they're told
To move the heart, and move it toward an ending,
To keep the pages turning to the back,

Dickens on Fire

(Not to imply his urgent fluency
Spared him the chosen trials of the trade,
    The fundamental restlessness,
        Dead hours, dead days, dead weeks,
    The sharp downspirals of depression
        And pained uncertainty,
The getting up then coming back to see
        What little mess
        We've made
    Or haven't, the obsession
    Guttering till our dark distress
    Snuffs out another hapless session
        Where more is less,
When skies clear, from the valleys rise the peaks,
The dam breaks and the images cascade),

Then stop for lunch, done writing for the day
At two or three, and after a hearty feed
    Launch vigorous activity,
        A long and fast-paced walk
    Through fields and lanes, or streets and parks,
    Then home to, fiercely, play
At cricket, pocket billiards, or croquet,
        And after tea
        Proceed
    With more communal larks,
    As brisk conviviality
    Strikes brilliant conversational sparks,
        Civility
Brings drink and food and funny games and talk
All wreathed in smoke, according to his need,

Dickens on Fire

Or, if he had the numbers, organize
His family and friends into a troupe
    To take a part and break a leg
        For dramaturgic purpose,
    Staging whatever he'd select
        While he would scrutinize
 And drill the children, prompt and tyrannize
           (But never beg)
        The group
    To quickening effect,
    As he, both fuse and powder keg,
    Would blaze away, and thus infect
          Augustus Egg
And Forster and Frank Stone and Uncle Porpoise
Till they would conquer, since they must not stoop,

Or drop by places where he'd find his friends,
The Athenaeum, or the Parthenon,
    The Garrick, where the smoke was thick
        And he could have his say
    Among the clubby tight connections
        Frank *bonhomie* extends,
Denounce what someone mindlessly defends
        Or parry *Sic*
          Et Non,
    Discuss the next elections,
    The latest play, the lunatic
    Love-muddled slapstick indirections
        Of some sidekick
As, effervescent, wired, on high display,
The Sparkler sparkled evenings, on and on,

Or supervise a testimonial
Dinner to benefit some heartfelt cause,
    Old actors or the Ragged Schools,
        Reforming prostitutes,
    Clean water and less filthy air
        (His ceremonial
Issues were native, not colonial),
           To torch the fools'
        Dumb laws
        (Sunday restrictions) where
    Flammable, drain the worst cesspools,
    Build decent housing (Columbia Square),
        Rhetorical tools
Full bore, "Thanks to you all, thanks to Miss Coutts,"
A last drumroll, the punchline, the applause,

Though for long stretches he would spend his days
On one consuming project (still in his prime,
    Or so he thought, strength could be found,
        Plus he had many bills),
    Like editing a magazine
        For fiction, reviews of plays,
Opinionated letters, brave essays
        To clear the ground,
           The grime,
    The soot, to fix the scene,
So *Household Words*, then *All the Year Round*
Would flash together, burnished clean
        And market-bound,
With help from his assistant, W. H. Wills,
Another number, ship-shape, out on time,

Dickens on Fire

Or dragging his Dramatic Company
On tour again (no other thrill would suffice—
    He missed the stage lights, burned to go,
        And tickets always sold
    For amateur theatricals
        Where a happy few could see
A cast of odd, esteemed celebrity
          Braving the snow
        And ice
    To not turn cannibals
Despite *The Frozen Deep*), just so
    Feeling would fill the meeting halls
        And only grow
To warm his Wardour, dying in the cold,
Rapt with the ardors of self-sacrifice,

And then there were the constant public readings
That drove and drained him through his latter years,
    So lucrative, he would insist
        He must go on despite
    Exhaustion, bravely take the stage
        For ritual proceedings
(Doctors objected, he ignored their pleadings,
        Proudly dismissed
          Their fears),
    The great man of the age
    A spectacle (as he'd persist
    The characters leapt off the page)
        Not to be missed,
The desk, the hat, the gloves, the even light,
The sure crescendo, the held breath, the cheers,

All so addictive, apple of every eye,
Charley was their darling, he was adored,
    They found it riveting, sublime,
        Loved the trial in *Pickwick*,
    Loved to pity the little tykes
        Like Copperfield, whose "I"
Was him, and Tiny Tim, "who did NOT die"
            This Christmastime
                (They roared),
        Shuddered in fear when Sikes
    Would finish Nancy one more time
    (She pleads, he lifts the club, he strikes,
            He flees the crime)
As, murderer and murdered, he felt sick,
His body suffered as their spirits soared,

Then, too, because of or despite it all,
The man was always moving, in nervous flight
    From boredom or mortality,
        To witness, sundry-wise,
    The elemental earthly show,
        Summoned by the call
Of roaring water to watch Niagara fall
        All majesty
            And might
        Shimmer-spanned by rainbow
    After rainbow, ceaselessly
    Crashing a hundred feet below,
            Where he could see
Tremendous ghosts of spray and mist arise,
Veils of the first things, darkness, depth, God, light,

Or drawn to clamber, one sharp winter night,
Accompanied by guides, his pregnant wife,
    Georgina, "Pickle," a fat stranger,
        Up Mount Vesuvius,
    Intentionally starting late
      To climb in fading light
(He timed it to the moonrise, it was tight)
        Despite all danger
          To life
    And limb, as if dumb fate
  Were some benevolent arranger,
    Though told they really shouldn't wait
      He wouldn't change or
Waver, pressed on ("Good Lord deliver us,"
The sherpas prayed) as wind cut like a knife,

The litters with the women in them veered,
The porters stumbled, cursing, shrieked advice,
    The fat man's litter wobbled, hovered,
      While, creeping, up they went
(Descent posed the real risk of falling,
      When Pickle disappeared,
Slipping right down a slope that, as he feared,
        Was slickly covered
          In ice,
    Wildly cannonballing
  Out of sight, to be recovered),
    Up where a smoke-filled, sulfurous, appalling
      Plain discovered
Gigantic cinders, with flakes of fire, hell-sent,
Rained down to scorch an anti-paradise,

Dickens on Fire

And where great sheets of flame streamed forth he must,
True to his own wild way, rashly ascend
    To see the molten crater churning,
        Must crawl right to the brim
    And, singeing, linger there (although
        He found having to trust
His weight to the thinness of the trembling crust
        A touch concerning),
           Suspend-
      ed, boiling gulf below,
    Then, giddy, roll back down, returning
    Blackened, smoking from head to toe,
        His clothes still burning,
But all in every moment, being him,
Dickens on fire, as always, right to the end.

A Note About the Author

Photo courtesy of Rob Crandall © 2019

Joseph Harrison was born in Richmond, Virginia, grew up in Virginia and Alabama, and took degrees at Yale and Johns Hopkins. He is the author of five previous books of poetry, including *Someone Else's Name* (2003), *Identity Theft* (2008), and *Shakespeare's Horse* (2015). *Someone Else's Name* was named one of five poetry books of the year by *The Washington Post* and was a finalist for the Poets' Prize; *Shakespeare's Horse* was also a finalist for the Poets' Prize. He has received a Guggenheim fellowship in poetry and an Academy Award in Literature from the American Academy of Arts and Letters, among other honors.

Mr. Harrison has directed the Anthony Hecht Poetry Prize since its inception in 2006. He edited *The Hecht Prize Anthology* (2010) and, with Damiano Abeni, *Un mondo che non può essere migliore* (2008), a selection from the poetry of John Ashbery that won a Special Prize from the Premio Napoli. He lives in Baltimore, where he teaches privately and works as an editor.

Other Books from Waywiser

POETRY

Austin Allen, *Pleasures of the Game*
Al Alvarez, *New & Selected Poems*
Chris Andrews, *Lime Green Chair*
Audrey Bohanan, *Any Keep or Contour*
George Bradley, *A Few of Her Secrets*
Geoffrey Brock, *Voices Bright Flags*
Christopher Cessac, *The Youngest Ocean*
Robert Conquest, *Blokelore & Blokesongs*
Robert Conquest, *Collected Poems*
Robert Conquest, *Penultimata*
Morri Creech, *Blue Rooms*
Morri Creech, *Field Knowledge*
Morri Creech, *The Sleep of Reason*
Peter Dale, *One Another*
Erica Dawson, *Big-Eyed Afraid*
B. H. Fairchild, *The Art of the Lathe*
David Ferry, *On This Side of the River: Selected Poems*
Daniel Groves & Greg Williamson, eds., *Jiggery-Pokery Semicentennial*
Jeffrey Harrison, *The Names of Things: New & Selected Poems*
Joseph Harrison, *Identity Theft*
Joseph Harrison, *Shakespeare's Horse*
Joseph Harrison, *Someone Else's Name*
Joseph Harrison, ed., *The Hecht Prize Anthology, 2005-2009*
Anthony Hecht, *Collected Later Poems*
Anthony Hecht, *The Darkness and the Light*
Jaimee Hills, *How to Avoid Speaking*
Katherine Hollander, *My German Dictionary*
Hilary S. Jacqmin, *Missing Persons*
Carrie Jerrell, *After the Revival*
Stephen Kampa, *Articulate as Rain*
Stephen Kampa, *Bachelor Pad*
Rose Kelleher, *Bundle o' Tinder*
Mark Kraushaar, *The Uncertainty Principle*
Matthew Ladd, *The Book of Emblems*
J. D. McClatchy, *Plundered Hearts: New and Selected Poems*
Dora Malech, *Shore Ordered Ocean*
Jérôme Luc Martin, *The Gardening Fires: Sonnets and Fragments*
Eric McHenry, *Odd Evening*
Eric McHenry, *Potscrubber Lullabies*
Eric McHenry and Nicholas Garland, *Mommy Daddy Evan Sage*
Timothy Murphy, *Very Far North*
Ian Parks, *Shell Island*
V. Penelope Pelizzon, *Whose Flesh is Flame, Whose Bone is Time*
Chris Preddle, *Cattle Console Him*
Shelley Puhak, *Guinevere in Baltimore*

Other Books from Waywiser

Christopher Ricks, ed., *Joining Music with Reason:*
34 Poets, British and American, Oxford 2004-2009
Daniel Rifenburgh, *Advent*
Mary Jo Salter, *It's Hard to Say: Selected Poems*
W. D. Snodgrass, *Not for Specialists: New & Selected Poems*
Mark Strand, *Almost Invisible*
Mark Strand, *Blizzard of One*
Bradford Gray Telford, *Perfect Hurt*
Matthew Thorburn, *This Time Tomorrow*
Cody Walker, *Shuffle and Breakdown*
Cody Walker, *The Self-Styled No-Child*
Cody Walker, *The Trumpiad*
Deborah Warren, *The Size of Happiness*
Clive Watkins, *Already the Flames*
Clive Watkins, *Jigsaw*
Richard Wilbur, *Anterooms*
Richard Wilbur, *Mayflies*
Richard Wilbur, *Collected Poems 1943-2004*
Norman Williams, *One Unblinking Eye*
Greg Williamson, *A Most Marvelous Piece of Luck*
Greg Williamson, *The Hole Story of Kirby the Sneak and Arlo the True*
Stephen Yenser, *Stone Fruit*

FICTION
Gregory Heath, *The Entire Animal*
Mary Elizabeth Pope, *Divining Venus*
K. M. Ross, *The Blinding Walk*
Gabriel Roth, *The Unknowns**
Matthew Yorke, *Chancing It*

ILLUSTRATED
Nicholas Garland, *I wish ...*
Eric McHenry and Nicholas Garland, *Mommy Daddy Evan Sage*
Greg Williamson, *The Hole Story of Kirby the Sneak and Arlo the True*

NON-FICTION
Neil Berry, *Articles of Faith: The Story of British Intellectual Journalism*
Irving Feldman, *Usable Truths: Aphorisms & Observations*
Mark Ford, *A Driftwood Altar: Essays and Reviews*
Philip Hoy, ed., *A Bountiful Harvest:*
The Correspondence of Anthony Hecht and William L. MacDonald
Richard Wollheim, *Germs: A Memoir of Childhood*

* Co-published with Picador